Compost

Written by
Cath Jones

I am Bran.

You will see me in a compost bin.

You might ask, "What is compost?"

Look. This is compost.

Compost has lots of good food for plants in it.

This is my compost bin.

A good compost bin has lots of living things like me in it.

We turn **organic matter** into good compost. Munch, chomp slurp!

But we need to be kept dark and moist.

Bright sunlight? No thank you!

What can you add to a compost bin?

 Farmyard manure

 Pet poo and pet bedding (but not cat poo or dog poo!)

 Weeds

 Card

Little bits of tree, such as conifer clippings

Wood ash

Wool

Hair

You cannot compost: metal cans, plastic, or ash from coal.

When you cook, pop the peel and scraps in the compost bin.

It is good for getting rid of them.

They will rot down and turn into fantastic compost.

Adding some green garden rubbish helps the compost to rot and is better than burning it.

Composting is so good for the planet.

When you compost, less rubbish ends up in landfill.

Mix the compost from the bin into the soil and turn it with a fork.

Or you can just add it on top of the soil. This is a **mulch**.

It is so good for the soil.

This is a compost tumbler. You turn it to mix the compost. It is so quick: you get compost in 3 or 4 weeks. Smart!

A compost bin can be free.

You can nail pallets together. This is a good compost bin.

But do not forget: you must turn the compost with a fork.

This is a compost toilet.

Now this is clever! You wee and poo, then add wood chippings.

When it all rots down, you get fantastic compost.

Composting is so cool! It is free to do and is so good for the planet.

Start composting now!